UNIVERSAL DECLARATION OF HUMAN RIGHTS

Universal Declaration

OF
Human Rights
in
English
Spanish
French
Chinese
Russian
Arabic

ELEANOR ROOSEVELT et al.

APPLEWOOD BOOKS
Carlisle, Massachusetts

Thank you for purchasing an Applewood Book.
Applewood reprints America's lively classics—books from
the past that are still of interest to modern readers. For a
free copy of our current catalog, please write to
Applewood Books, P.O. Box 27, Carlisle, MA 01741.

ISBN 978-1-55709-455-1

10

Printed in the U.S.A.

Universal Declaration of Human Rights

Preamble

Whereas recognition of the inherent dignity and of the equal and inalienable rights of all members of the human family is the foundation of freedom, justice and peace in the world,

Whereas disregard and contempt for human rights have resulted in barbarous acts which have outraged the conscience of mankind, and the advent of a world in which human beings shall enjoy freedom of speech and belief and freedom from fear and want has been proclaimed as the highest aspiration of the common people,

Whereas it is essential, if man is not to be compelled to have recourse, as a last resort, to rebellion against tyranny and oppression, that human rights should be protected by the rule of law,

Whereas it is essential to promote the development of friendly relations between nations,

Whereas the peoples of the United Nations have in the Charter reaffirmed their faith in fundamental human rights, in the dignity and worth of the human person and in the equal rights of men and women and have determined to promote social progress and better standards of life in larger freedom,

Whereas Member States have pledged themselves to achieve, in cooperation with the United Nations, the promotion of universal respect for and observance of human rights and fundamental freedoms,

Whereas a common understanding of these rights and freedoms is of the greatest importance for the full realization of this pledge,

Now, therefore,

The General Assembly

Proclaims this Universal Declaration of Human Rights as a common standard of achievement for all peoples and all nations, to the end that every individual and every organ of society, keeping this Declaration constantly in mind, shall strive by teaching and education to promote respect for these rights and freedoms and by progressive measures, national and international, to secure their universal and effective recognition and observance, both among the peoples of Member States themselves and among the peoples of territories under their jurisdiction.

Article I

All human beings are born free and equal in dignity and rights. They are endowed with reason and conscience and should act towards one another in a spirit of brotherhood.

Article 2

Everyone is entitled to all the rights and freedoms set forth in this Declaration, without distinction of any kind, such as race, colour, sex, language, religion, political or other opinion, national or social origin, property, birth or other status.

Furthermore, no distinction shall be made on the basis of the political, jurisdictional or international status of the country or territory to which a person belongs, whether it be independent, trust, non-self-governing or under any other limitation of sovereignty.

Article 3

Everyone has the right to life, liberty and security of person.

Article 4
No one shall be held in slavery or servitude; slavery and the slave trade shall be prohibited in all their forms.

Article 5
No one shall be subjected to torture or to cruel, inhuman or degrading treatment or punishment.

Article 6
Everyone has the right to recognition everywhere as a person before the law.

Article 7
All are equal before the law and are entitled without any discrimination to equal protection of the law. All are entitled to equal protection against any discrimination in violation of this Declaration and against any incitement to such discrimination.

Article 8
Everyone has the right to an effective remedy by the competent national tribunals for acts violating the fundamental right granted him by the constitution or by law.

Article 9
No one shall be subjected to arbitrary arrest, detention or exile.

Article 10
Everyone is entitled in full equality to a fair and public hearing by an independent and impartial tribunal, in the determination of his rights and obligations and of any criminal charge against him.

Article 11

1. Everyone charged with a penal offence has the right to be presumed innocent until proved guilty according to law in a public trial at which he has had all the guarantees necessary for his defence.

2. No one shall be held guilty of any penal offence on account of any act or omission which did not constitute a penal offence, under national or international law, at the time when it was committed. Nor shall a heavier penalty be imposed than the one that was applicable at the time the penal offence was committed.

Article 12

No one shall be subjected to arbitrary interference with his privacy, family, home or correspondence, nor to attacks upon his honour and reputation. Everyone has the right to the protection of the law against such interference or attacks.

Article 13

1. Everyone has the right to freedom of movement and residence within the borders of each State.

2. Everyone has the right to leave any country, including his own, and to return to his country.

Article 14

1. Everyone has the right to seek and to enjoy in other countries asylum from persecution.

2. This right may not be invoked in the case of prosecutions genuinely arising from non-political crimes or from acts contrary to the purposes and principles of the United Nations.

Article 15

1. Everyone has the right to a nationality.

2. No one shall be arbitrarily deprived of his nationality nor denied the right to change his nationality.

Article 16

1. Men and women of full age, without any limitation due to race, nationality or religion, have the right to marry and to found a family. They are entitled to equal rights as to marriage, during marriage and at its dissolution.

2. Marriage shall be entered into only with the free and full consent of the intending spouses.

3. The family is the natural and fundamental group unit of society and is entitled to protection by society and the State.

Article 17

1. Everyone has the right to own property alone as well as in association with others.

2. No one shall be arbitrarily deprived of his property.

Article 18

Everyone has the right to freedom of thought, conscience and religion; this right includes freedom to change his religion or belief, and freedom, either alone or in community with others and in public or private, to manifest his religion or belief in teaching, practice, worship and observance.

Article 19

Everyone has the right to freedom of opinion and expression; this right includes freedom to hold opinions without interference and to seek, receive and impart information and ideas through any media and regardless of frontiers.

Article 20

1. Everyone has the right to freedom of peaceful assembly and association.

2. No one may be compelled to belong to an association.

Article 21

1. Everyone has the right to take part in the government of his country, directly or through freely chosen representatives.

2. Everyone has the right to equal access to public service in his country.

3. The will of the people shall be the basis of the authority of government; this will shall be expressed in periodic and genuine elections which shall be by universal and equal suffrage and shall be held by secret vote or by equivalent free voting procedures.

Article 22

Everyone, as a member of society, has the right to social security and is entitled to realization, through national effort and international co-operation and in accordance with the organization and resources of each State, of the economic, social and cultural rights indispensable for his dignity and the free development of his personality.

Article 23

1. Everyone has the right to work, to free choice of employment, to just and favourable conditions of work and to protection against unemployment.

2. Everyone, without any discrimination, has the right to equal pay for equal work.

3. Everyone who works has the right to just and favourable remuneration ensuring for himself and his family an existence worthy of human dignity, and supplemented, if necessary, by other means of social protection.

4. Everyone has the right to form and to join trade unions for the protection of his interests.

Article 24

Everyone has the right to rest and leisure, including reasonable limitation of working hours and periodic holidays with pay.

Article 25

1. Everyone has the right to a standard of living adequate for the health and well-being of himself and of his family, including food, clothing, housing and medical care and necessary social services, and the right to security in the event of unemployment, sickness, disability, widowhood, old age or other lack of livelihood in circumstances beyond his control.

2. Motherhood and childhood are entitled to special care and assistance. All children, whether born in or out of wedlock, shall enjoy the same social protection.

Article 26

1. Everyone has the right to education. Education shall be free, at least in the elementary and fundamental stages. Elementary education shall be compulsory. Technical and professional education shall be made generally available and higher education shall be equally accessible to all on the basis of merit.

2. Education shall be directed to the full development of the human personality and to the strengthening

of respect for human rights and fundamental freedoms. It shall promote understanding, tolerance and friendship among all nations, racial or religious groups, and shall further the activities of the United Nations for the maintenance of peace.

3. Parents have a prior right to choose the kind of education that shall be given to their children.

Article 27

1. Everyone has the right freely to participate in the cultural life of the community, to enjoy the arts and to share in scientific advancement and its benefits.

2. Everyone has the right to the protection of the moral and material interests resulting from any scientific, literary or artistic production of which he is the author.

Article 28

Everyone is entitled to a social and international order in which the rights and freedoms set forth in this Declaration can be fully realized.

Article 29

1. Everyone has duties to the community in which alone the free and full development of his personality is possible.

2. In the exercise of his rights and freedoms, everyone shall be subject only to such limitations as are determined by law solely for the purpose of securing due recognition and respect for the rights and freedoms of others and of meeting the just requirements of morality, public order and the general welfare in a democratic society.

3. These rights and freedoms may in no case be exercised contrary to the purposes and principles of the United Nations.

Article 30

Nothing in this Declaration may be interpreted as implying for any State, group or person any right to engage in any activity or to perform any act aimed at the destruction of any of the rights and freedoms set forth herein.

Declaración Universal de Derechos Humanos

Adoptada y proclamada por la Asamblea General en su resolución 217 A (III), de 10 de diciembre de 1948

Preámbulo

Considerando que la libertad, la justicia y la paz en el mundo tienen por base el reconocimiento de la dignidad intrínseca y de los derechos iguales e inalienables de todos los miembros de la familia humana,

Considerando que el desconocimiento y el menosprecio de los derechos humanos han originado actos de barbarie ultrajantes para la conciencia de la humanidad; y que se ha proclamado, como la aspiración más elevada del hombre, el advenimiento de un mundo en que los seres humanos, liberados del temor y de la miseria, disfruten de la libertad de palabra y de la libertad de creencias,

Considerando esencial que los derechos humanos sean protegidos por un régimen de Derecho, a fin de que el hombre no se vea compelido al supremo recurso de la rebelión contra la tiranía y la opresión,

Considerando también esencial promover el desarrollo de relaciones amistosas entre las naciones,

Considerando que los pueblos de las Naciones Unidas han reafirmado en la Carta su fe en los derechos fundamentales del hombre, en la dignidad y el valor de la persona humana y en la igualdad de derechos de hombres y mujeres; y se han declarado resueltos a promover el progreso social y a elevar el nivel de vida dentro de un concepto más amplio de la libertad,

Considerando que los Estados Miembros se han comprometido a asegurar, en cooperación con la Organización de las Naciones Unidas, el respeto universal y efectivo a los derechos y libertades fundamentales del hombre, y

Considerando que una concepción común de estos derechos y libertades es de la mayor importancia para el pleno cumplimiento de dicho compromiso,

La Asamblea General

Proclama la presente Declaración Universal de Derechos Humanos como ideal común por el que todos los pueblos y naciones deben esforzarse, a fin de que tanto los individuos como las instituciones, inspirándose constantemente en ella, promuevan, mediante la enseñanza y la educación, el respeto a estos derechos y libertades, y aseguren, por medidas progresivas de carácter nacional e internacional, su reconocimiento y aplicación universales y efectivos, tanto entre los pueblos de los Estados Miembros como entre los de los territorios colocados bajo su jurisdicción.

Artículo 1

Todos los seres humanos nacen libres e iguales en dignidad y derechos y, dotados como están de razón y conciencia, deben comportarse fraternalmente los unos con los otros.

Artículo 2

Toda persona tiene los derechos y libertades proclamados en esta Declaración, sin distinción alguna de raza, color, sexo, idioma, religión, opinión política o de cualquier otra índole, origen nacional o social, posición económica, nacimiento o cualquier otra condición.

Además, no se hará distinción alguna fundada en la condición política, jurídica o internacional del país o territorio de cuya jurisdicción dependa una persona, tanto si se trata de un país independiente, como de un territorio bajo administración fiduciaria, no autónomo o sometido a cualquier otra limitación de soberanía.

Artículo 3

Todo individuo tiene derecho a la vida, a la libertad y a la seguridad de su persona.

Artículo 4

Nadie estará sometido a esclavitud ni a servidumbre; la esclavitud y la trata de esclavos están prohibidas en todas sus formas.

Artículo 5

Nadie será sometido a torturas ni a penas o tratos crueles, inhumanos o degradantes.

Artículo 6

Todo ser humano tiene derecho, en todas partes, al reconocimiento de su personalidad jurídica.

Artículo 7

Todos son iguales ante la ley y tienen, sin distinción, derecho a igual protección de la ley. Todos tienen derecho a igual protección contra toda discriminación que infrinja esta Declaración y contra toda provocación a tal discriminación.

Artículo 8

Toda persona tiene derecho a un recurso efectivo, ante los tribunales nacionales competentes, que la ampare contra actos que violen sus derechos fundamentales reconocidos por la constitución o por la ley.

Artículo 9

Nadie podrá ser arbitrariamente detenido, preso ni desterrado.

Artículo 10

Toda persona tiene derecho, en condiciones de plena

igualdad, a ser oída públicamente y con justicia por un tribunal independiente e imparcial, para la determinación de sus derechos y obligaciones o para el examen de cualquier acusación contra ella en materia penal.

Artículo 11

1. Toda persona acusada de delito tiene derecho a que se presuma su inocencia mientras no se pruebe su culpabilidad, conforme a la ley y en juicio público en el que se le hayan asegurado todas las garantías necesarias para su defensa.

2. Nadie será condenado por actos u omisiones que en el momento de cometerse no fueron delictivos según el Derecho nacional o internacional. Tampoco se impondrá pena más grave que la aplicable en el momento de la comisión del delito.

Artículo 12

Nadie será objeto de injerencias arbitrarias en su vida privada, su familia, su domicilio o su correspondencia, ni de ataques a su honra o a su reputación. Toda persona tiene derecho a la protección de la ley contra tales injerencias o ataques.

Artículo 13

1. Toda persona tiene derecho a circular libremente y a elegir su residencia en el territorio de un Estado.

2. Toda persona tiene derecho a salir de cualquier país, incluso el propio, y a regresar a su país.

Artículo 14

1. En caso de persecución, toda persona tiene derecho a buscar asilo, y a disfrutar de él, en cualquier país.

2. Este derecho no podrá ser invocado contra una acción judicial realmente originada por delitos comunes o por actos opuestos a los propósitos y principios de las Naciones Unidas.

Artículo 15

1. Toda persona tiene derecho a una nacionalidad.

2. A nadie se privará arbitrariamente de su nacionalidad ni del derecho a cambiar de nacionalidad.

Artículo 16

1. Los hombres y las mujeres, a partir de la edad núbil, tienen derecho, sin restricción alguna por motivos de raza, nacionalidad o religión, a casarse y fundar una familia; y disfrutarán de iguales derechos en cuanto al matrimonio, durante el matrimonio y en caso de disolución del matrimonio.

2. Sólo mediante libre y pleno consentimiento de los futuros esposos podrá contraerse el matrimonio.

3. La familia es el elemento natural y fundamental de la sociedad y tiene derecho a la protección de la sociedad y del Estado.

Artículo 17

1. Toda persona tiene derecho a la propiedad, individual y colectivamente.

2. Nadie será privado arbitrariamente de su propiedad.

Artículo 18

Toda persona tiene derecho a la libertad de pensamiento, de conciencia y de religión; este derecho incluye la libertad de cambiar de religión o de creencia, así como la libertad de manifestar su religión o su creencia, individual y colectivamente, tanto en público como en privado, por la enseñanza, la práctica, el culto y la observancia.

Artículo 19

Todo individuo tiene derecho a la libertad de opinión y de expresión; este derecho incluye el no ser molestado a causa de sus opiniones, el de investigar y recibir informaciones y opiniones, y el de difundirlas, sin limitación de fronteras, por cualquier medio de expresión.

Artículo 20

1. Toda persona tiene derecho a la libertad de reunión y de asociación pacíficas.

2. Nadie podrá ser obligado a pertenecer a una asociación.

Artículo 21

1. Toda persona tiene derecho a participar en el gobierno de su país, directamente o por medio de representantes libremente escogidos.

2. Toda persona tiene el derecho de acceso, en condiciones de igualdad, a las funciones públicas de su país.

3. La voluntad del pueblo es la base de la autoridad del poder público; esta voluntad se expresará mediante elecciones auténticas que habrán de celebrarse periódicamente, por sufragio universal e igual y por voto secreto u otro procedimiento equivalente que garantice la libertad del voto.

Artículo 22

Toda persona, como miembro de la sociedad, tiene derecho a la seguridad social, y a obtener, mediante el esfuerzo nacional y la cooperación internacional, habida cuenta de la organización y los recursos de cada Estado, la satisfacción de los derechos económicos, sociales y culturales, indispensables a su dignidad y al libre desarrollo de su personalidad.

Artículo 23

1. Toda persona tiene derecho al trabajo, a la libre elección de su trabajo, a condiciones equitativas y satisfactorias de trabajo y a la protección contra el desempleo.

2. Toda personal tiene derecho, sin discriminación alguna, a igual salario por trabajo igual.

3. Toda persona que trabaja tiene derecho a una remuneración equitativa y satisfactoria, que le asegure, así como a su familia, una existencia conforme a la dignidad humana y

que será completada, en caso necesario, por cualesquiera otros medios de protección social.

4. Toda persona tiene derecho a fundar sindicatos y a sindicarse para la defensa de sus intereses.

Artículo 24

Toda persona tiene derecho al descanso, al disfrute del tiempo libre, a una limitación razonable de la duración del trabajo y a vacaciones periódicas pagadas.

Artículo 25

1. Toda persona tiene derecho a un nivel de vida adecuado que le asegure, así como a su familia, la salud y el bienestar, y en especial la alimentación, el vestido, la vivienda, la asistencia médica y los servicios sociales necesarios; tiene asimismo derecho a los seguros en caso de desempleo, enfermedad, invalidez, viudez, vejez y otros casos de pérdida de sus medios de subsistencia por circunstancias independientes de su voluntad.

2. La maternidad y la infancia tienen derecho a cuidados y asistencia especiales. Todos los niños, nacidos de matrimonio o fuera de matrimonio, tienen derecho a igual protección social.

Artículo 26

1. Toda persona tiene derecho a la educación. La educación debe ser gratuita, al menos en lo concerniente a la instrucción elemental y fundamental. La instrucción elemental será obligatoria. La instrucción técnica y profesional habrá de ser generalizada; el acceso a los estudios superiores será igual para todos, en función de los méritos respectivos.

2. La educación tendrá por objeto el pleno desarrollo de la personalidad humana y el fortalecimiento del respeto a los derechos humanos y a las libertades fundamentales; favorecerá la comprensión, la tolerancia y la amistad entre todas las

naciones y todos los grupos étnicos o religiosos; y promoverá el desarrollo de las actividades de las Naciones Unidas para el mantenimiento de la paz.

3. Los padres tendrán derecho preferente a escoger el tipo de educación que habrá de darse a sus hijos.

Artículo 27

1. Toda persona tiene derecho a tomar parte libremente en la vida cultural de la comunidad, a gozar de las artes y a participar en el progreso científico y en los beneficios que de él resulten.

2. Toda persona tiene derecho a la protección de los intereses morales y materiales que le correspondan por razón de las producciones científicas, literarias o artísticas de que sea autora.

Artículo 28

Toda persona tiene derecho a que se establezca un orden social e internacional en el que los derechos y libertades proclamados en esta Declaración se hagan plenamente efectivos.

Artículo 29

1. Toda persona tiene deberes respecto a la comunidad, puesto que sólo en ella puede desarrollar libre y plenamente su personalidad.

2. En el ejercicio de sus derechos y en el disfrute de sus libertades, toda persona estará solamente sujeta a las limitaciones establecidas por la ley con el único fin de asegurar el reconocimiento y el respeto de los derechos y libertades de los demás, y de satisfacer las justas exigencias de la moral, del orden público y del bienestar general en una sociedad democrática.

3. Estos derechos y libertades no podrán en ningún caso ser ejercidos en oposición a los propósitos y principios de las Naciones Unidas.

Artículo 30

Nada en la presente Declaración podrá interpretarse en el sentido de que confiere derecho alguno al Estado, a un grupo o a una persona, para emprender y desarrollar actividades o realizar actos tendientes a la supresión de cualquiera de los derechos y libertades proclamados en esta Declaración.

Déclaration universelle des droits de l'homme

Préambule

Considérant que la reconnaissance de la dignité inhérente à tous les membres de la famille humaine et de leurs droits égaux et inaliénables constitue le fondement de la liberté, de la justice et de la paix dans le monde,

Considérant que la méconnaissance et le mépris des droits de l'homme ont conduit à des actes de barbarie qui révoltent la conscience de l'humanité et que l'avènement d'un monde où les êtres humains seront libres de parler et de croire, libérés de la terreur et de la misère, a été proclamé comme la plus haute aspiration de l'homme,

Considérant qu'il est essentiel que les droits de l'homme soient protégés par un régime de droit pour que l'homme ne soit pas contraint, en suprême recours, à la révolte contre la tyrannie et l'oppression,

Considérant qu'il est essentiel d'encourager le développement de relations amicales entre nations,

Considérant que dans la Charte les peuples des Nations Unies ont proclamé à nouveau leur foi dans les droits fondamentaux de l'homme, dans la dignité et la valeur de la personne humaine, dans l'égalité des droits des hommes et des femmes, et qu'ils se sont déclarés résolus à favoriser le progrès social et à instaurer de meilleures conditions de vie dans une liberté plus grande,

Considérant que les Etats Membres se sont engagés à assurer, en coopération avec l'Organisation des Nations Unies, le respect universel et effectif des droits de l'homme et des libertés fondamentales,

Considérant qu'une conception commune de ces droits et libertés est de la plus haute importance pour remplir pleinement cet engagement,

L'Assemblée générale

Proclame la présente Déclaration universelle des droits de l'homme comme l'idéal commun à atteindre par tous les peuples et toutes les nations afin que tous les individus et tous les organes de la société, ayant cette Déclaration constamment à l'esprit, s'efforcent, par l'enseignement et l'éducation, de développer le respect de ces droits et libertés et d'en assurer, par des mesures progressives d'ordre national et international, la reconnaissance et l'application universelles et effectives, tant parmi les populations des Etats Membres eux-mêmes que parmi celles des territoires placés sous leur juridiction.

Article premier

Tous les êtres humains naissent libres et égaux en dignité et en droits. Ils sont doués de raison et de conscience et doivent agir les uns envers les autres dans un esprit de fraternité.

Article 2

Chacun peut se prévaloir de tous les droits et de toutes les libertés proclamés dans la présente Déclaration, sans distinction aucune, notamment de race, de couleur, de sexe, de langue, de religion, d'opinion politique ou de toute autre opinion, d'origine nationale ou sociale, de fortune, de naissance ou de toute autre situation.

De plus, il ne sera fait aucune distinction fondée sur le statut politique, juridique ou international du pays ou du territoire dont une personne est ressortissante, que ce pays ou territoire soit indépendant, sous tutelle, non autonome ou soumis à une limitation quelconque de souveraineté.

Article 3

Tout individu a droit à la vie, à la liberté et à la sûreté de sa personne.

Article 4

Nul ne sera tenu en esclavage ni en servitude; l'esclavage et la traite des esclaves sont interdits sous toutes leurs formes.

Article 5

Nul ne sera soumis à la torture, ni à des peines ou traitements cruels, inhumains ou dégradants.

Article 6

Chacun a le droit à la reconnaissance en tous lieux de sa personnalité juridique.

Article 7

Tous sont égaux devant la loi et ont droit sans distinction à une égale protection de la loi. Tous ont droit à une protection égale contre toute discrimination qui violerait la présente Déclaration et contre toute provocation à une telle discrimination.

Article 8

Toute personne a droit à un recours effectif devant les juridictions nationales compétentes contre les actes violant les droits fondamentaux qui lui sont reconnus par la constitution ou par la loi.

Article 9

Nul ne peut être arbitrairement arrêté, détenu ni exilé.

Article 10

Toute personne a droit, en pleine égalité, à ce que sa cause soit entendue équitablement et publiquement par un tribunal indépendant et impartial, qui décidera, soit de ses droits et obligations, soit du bien-fondé de toute accusation en matière pénale dirigée contre elle.

Article 11

1. Toute personne accusée d'un acte délictueux est présumée innocente jusqu'à ce que sa culpabilité ait été légalement établie au cours d'un procès public où toutes les garanties nécessaires à sa défense lui auront été assurées.

2. Nul ne sera condamné pour des actions ou omissions qui, au moment où elles ont été commises, ne constituaient pas un acte délictueux d'après le droit national ou international. De même, il ne sera infligé aucune peine plus forte que celle qui était applicable au moment où l'acte délictueux a été commis.

Article 12

Nul ne sera l'objet d'immixtions arbitraires dans sa vie privée, sa famille, son domicile ou sa correspondance, ni d'atteintes à son honneur et à sa réputation. Toute personne a droit à la protection de la loi contre de telles immixtions ou de telles atteintes.

Article 13

1. Toute personne a le droit de circuler librement et de choisir sa résidence à l'intérieur d'un Etat.

2. Toute personne a le droit de quitter tout pays, y compris le sien, et de revenir dans son pays.

Article 14

1. Devant la persécution, toute personne a le droit de chercher asile et de bénéficier de l'asile en d'autres pays.

2. Ce droit ne peut être invoqué dans le cas de poursuites réellement fondées sur un crime de droit commun ou sur des agissements contraires aux buts et aux principes des Nations Unies.

Article 15

1. Tout individu a droit à une nationalité.

2. Nul ne peut être arbitrairement privé de sa nationalité, ni du droit de changer de nationalité.

Article 16

1. A partir de l'âge nubile, l'homme et la femme, sans aucune restriction quant à la race, la nationalité ou la religion, ont le droit de se marier et de fonder une famille. Ils ont des droits égaux au regard du mariage, durant le mariage et lors de sa dissolution.

2. Le mariage ne peut être conclu qu'avec le libre et plein consentement des futurs époux.

3. La famille est l'élément naturel et fondamental de la société et a droit à la protection de la société et de l'Etat.

Article 17

1. Toute personne, aussi bien seule qu'en collectivité, a droit à la propriété.

2. Nul ne peut être arbitrairement privé de sa propriété.

Article 18

Toute personne a droit à la liberté de pensée, de conscience et de religion; ce droit implique la liberté de changer de religion ou de conviction ainsi que la liberté de manifester sa religion ou sa conviction, seule ou en commun, tant en public qu'en privé, par l'enseignement, les pratiques, le culte et l'accomplissement des rites.

Article 19

Tout individu a droit à la liberté d'opinion et d'expression, ce qui implique le droit de ne pas être inquiété pour ses opinions et celui de chercher, de recevoir et de répandre, sans considérations de frontières, les informations et les idées par quelque moyen d'expression que ce soit.

Article 20

1. Toute personne a droit à la liberté de réunion et d'association pacifiques.

2. Nul ne peut être obligé de faire partie d'une association.

Article 21

1. Toute personne a le droit de prendre part à la direction des affaires publiques de son pays, soit directement, soit par l'intermédiaire de représentants librement choisis.

2. Toute personne a droit à accéder, dans des conditions d'égalité, aux fonctions publiques de son pays.

3. La volonté du peuple est le fondement de l'autorité des pouvoirs publics; cette volonté doit s'exprimer par des élections honnêtes qui doivent avoir lieu périodiquement, au suffrage universel égal et au vote secret ou suivant une procédure équivalente assurant la liberté du vote.

Article 22

Toute personne, en tant que membre de la société, a droit à la sécurité sociale; elle est fondée à obtenir la satisfaction des droits économiques, sociaux et culturels indispensables à sa dignité et au libre développement de sa personnalité, grâce à l'effort national et à la coopération internationale, compte tenu de l'organisation et des ressources de chaque pays.

Article 23

1. Toute personne a droit au travail, au libre choix de son travail, à des conditions équitables et satisfaisantes de travail et à la protection contre le chômage.

2. Tous ont droit, sans aucune discrimination, à un salaire égal pour un travail égal.

3. Quiconque travaille a droit à une rémunération équitable et satisfaisante lui assurant ainsi qu'à sa famille une existence conforme à la dignité humaine et complétée, s'il y a lieu, par tous autres moyens de protection sociale.

4. Toute personne a le droit de fonder avec d'autres des syndicats et de s'affilier à des syndicats pour la défense de ses intérêts.

Article 24

Toute personne a droit au repos et aux loisirs et notamment à une limitation raisonnable de la durée du travail et à des congés payés périodiques.

Article 25

1. Toute personne a droit à un niveau de vie suffisant pour assurer sa santé, son bien-être et ceux de sa famille, notamment pour l'alimentation, l'habillement, le logement, les soins médicaux ainsi que pour les services sociaux nécessaires; elle a droit à la sécurité en cas de chômage, de maladie, d'invalidité, de veuvage, de vieillesse ou dans les autres cas de perte de ses moyens de subsistance par suite de circonstances indépendantes de sa volonté.

2. La maternité et l'enfance ont droit à une aide et à une assistance spéciales. Tous les enfants, qu'ils soient nés dans le mariage ou hors mariage, jouissent de la même protection sociale.

Article 26

1. Toute personne a droit à l'éducation. L'éducation doit être gratuite, au moins en ce qui concerne l'enseignement élémentaire et fondamental. L'enseignement élémentaire est obligatoire. L'enseignement technique et professionnel doit être généralisé; l'accès aux études supérieures doit être ouvert en pleine égalité à tous en fonction de leur mérite.

2. L'éducation doit viser au plein épanouissement de la personnalité humaine et au renforcement du respect des droits de l'homme et des libertés fondamentales. Elle doit favoriser la compréhension, la tolérance et l'amitié entre toutes les nations et tous les groupes raciaux ou religieux, ainsi que le développement des activités des Nations Unies pour le maintien de la paix.

3. Les parents ont, par priorité, le droit de choisir le genre d'éducation à donner à leurs enfants.

Article 27

1. Toute personne a le droit de prendre part librement à la vie culturelle de la communauté, de jouir des arts et de participer au progrès scientifique et aux bienfaits qui en résultent.

2. Chacun a droit à la protection des intérêts moraux et matériels découlant de toute production scientifique, littéraire ou artistique dont il est l'auteur.

Article 28

Toute personne a droit à ce que règne, sur le plan social et sur le plan international, un ordre tel que les droits et libertés énoncés dans la présente Déclaration puissent y trouver plein effet.

Article 29

1. L'individu a des devoirs envers la communauté dans laquelle seul le libre et plein développement de sa personnalité est possible.

2. Dans l'exercice de ses droits et dans la jouissance de ses libertés, chacun n'est soumis qu'aux limitations établies par la loi exclusivement en vue d'assurer la reconnaissance et le respect des droits et libertés d'autrui et afin de satisfaire aux justes exigences de la morale, de l'ordre public et du bien-être général dans une société démocratique.

3. Ces droits et libertés ne pourront, en aucun cas, s'exercer contrairement aux buts et aux principes des Nations Unies.

Article 30

Aucune disposition de la présente Déclaration ne peut être interprétée comme impliquant, pour un Etat, un groupement ou un individu, un droit quelconque de se livrer à une activité ou d'accomplir un acte visant à la destruction des droits et libertés qui y sont énoncés.

《世界人权宣言》[a]

序言

鉴于对人类家庭所有成员的固有尊严及其平等的和不移的权利的承认，乃是世界自由、正义与和平的基础，

鉴于对人权的无视和侮蔑已发展为野蛮暴行，这些暴行玷污了人类的良心，而一个人人享有言论和信仰自由并免于恐惧和匮乏的世界的来临，已被宣布为普通人民的最高愿望，

鉴于为使人类不致迫不得已铤而走险对暴政和压迫进行反叛，有必要使人权受法治的保护，

鉴于有必要促进各国间友好关系的发展，

鉴于各联合国国家的人民已在联合国宪章中重申他们对基本人权、人格尊严和价值以及男女平等权利的信念，并决心促成较大自由中的社会进步和生活水平的改善，

鉴于各会员国业已誓愿同联合国合作以促进对人权和基本自由的普遍尊重和遵行，

鉴于对这些权利和自由的普遍了解对于这个誓愿的充分实现具有很大的重要性，

因此现在，

大会，

---

a 经大会1948年12月10日第217A(III)号决议通过。

发布这一世界人权宣言，作为所有人民和所有国家努力实现的共同标准，以期每一个人和社会机构经常铭念本宣言，努力通过教诲和教育促进对权利和自由的尊重，并通过国家的和国际的渐进措施，使这些权利和自由在各会员国本身人民及在其管辖下领土的人民中得到普遍和有效的承认和遵行。

第一条

人人生而自由，在尊严和权利上一律平等。他们赋有理性和良心，并应以 兄弟关系的精神相对待。

第二条

人人有资格享受本宣言所载的一切权利和自由，不分种族、肤色、性别、 语言、宗教、政治或其他见解、国籍或社会出身、财产、出生或其他身份等任何 区别。

并且不得因一人所属的国家或领土的政治的、行政的或者国际的地位之不同而有所区别，无论该领土是独立领土、托管领土、非自治领土或者处于其他任何主权受限制的情况之下。

第三条

人人有权享有生命、自由和人生安全。

第四条

任何人不得使为奴隶或奴役；一切形式的奴隶制度和奴隶买卖，均应予以禁止。

第五条

任何人不得加以酷刑，或施以残忍的、不人道的或侮辱性的待遇或刑罚。

第六条

人人在任何地方有权被承认在法律前的人格。

第七条

法律之前人人平等，并有权享受法律的平等保护，不受任何歧视。人人有权享受平等保护，以免受违反本宣言的任何歧视行为以及煽动这种歧视的任何行为之害。

第八条

任何人当宪法或法律所赋予他的基本权利遭受侵害时，有权由合格的国家法庭对这种侵害行为作有效的补救。

第九条

任何人不得加以任何逮捕、拘禁或放逐。

第十条

人人完全平等地有权由一个独立而无偏倚的法庭进行公正的和公开的审讯，以确定他的权利和义务并判定对他提出的任何刑事指控。

第十一条

（一）凡受刑事控告者，在未经获得辩护上所需的一切保证的公开审判而依法证实有罪以前，有权被视为无罪。

（二）任何人的任何行为或不行为，在其发生时依国家法或国际法均不构成刑事罪者，不得被判为犯有刑事罪。刑罚不得重于犯罪时适用的法律规定。

第十二条

任何人的私生活、家庭、住宅和通信不得任意干涉，他的荣誉和名誉不得加以攻击。人人有权享受法律保护，以免受这种干涉或攻击。

第十三条

（一）人人在各国境内有权自由迁徙和居住。

（二）人人有权离开任何国家，包括其本国在内，并有权返回他的国家。

第十四条

（一）人人有权在其他国家寻求和享受庇护以避免迫害。

（二）在真正由于非政治性的罪行或违背联合国的宗旨和原则的行为而被起诉的情况下，不得援用此种权利。

第十五条

（一）人人有权享有国籍。

（二）任何人的国籍不得任意剥夺，亦不得否认其改变国籍的权利。

第十六条

（一）成年男女，不受种族、国籍或宗教的任何限制，有权婚嫁和成立 家庭。他们在婚姻方面，在结婚期间和在解除婚约时，应有平等权利。

（二）只有经男女双方的自由的和完全的同意，才能缔婚。

（三）家庭是天然的和基本的社会单元，并应受社会和国家的保护。

第十七条

（一）人人得有单独的财产所有权以及同他人合有的所有权。

（二）任何人的财产不得任意剥夺。

第十八条

人人有思想、良心和宗教自由的权利：此项权利包括改变他的宗教或信仰的自由，以及单独或集体、公开或秘密地以教义、实践、礼拜和戒律表示他的宗教或信仰的自由。

第十九条

人人有权享有主张和发表意见的自由：此项权利包括持有主张而不受干涉的自由，和通过任何媒介和不论国界寻求、接受和传递消息和思想的自由。

第二十条

（一）人人有权享有和平集会和结社的自由。

（二）任何人不得迫使隶属于某一团体。

第二十一条

（一）人人有直接或通过自由选择的代表参与治理本国的权利。

（二）人人有平等机会参加本国公务的权利。

（三）人民的意志是政府权利的基础；这一意志应以定期的和真正的选举予以表现，而选举应依据普遍和平等的投票权，并以不记名投票或相当的自由投票程序进行。

第二十二条

每个人，作为社会的一员，有权享受社会保障，并有权享受他的个人尊严和人格的自由发展所必需的经济、社会和文化方面各种权利的实现，这种实现是通过国家努力和国际合作并依照各国的组织和资源情况。

第二十三条

（一）人人有权工作、自由选择职业、享受公正和合适的工作条件并享受免于失业的保障。

（二）人人有同工同酬的权利，不受任何歧视。

（三）每一个工作的人，有权享受公正和合适的报酬，保证使他本人和家属有一个符合人的尊严的生活条件，必要时并辅以其他方式的社会保障。

（四）人人有为维护其利益而组织和参加工会的权利。

第二十四条

人人有享受休息和闲暇的权利，包括工作时间有合理限制和定期给薪休假的权利。

第二十五条

（一）人人有权享受为维持他本人和家属的健康和福利所需的生活水准，包括食物、衣著、住房、医疗和必要的社会服务；在遭到失业、疾病、残废、守寡、衰老或在其他不能控制的情况下丧失谋生能力时，有权享受保障。

（二）母亲和儿童有权享受特别照顾和协助。一切儿童，无论婚生或非婚 生，都应享受同样的社会保护。

第二十六条

（一）人人都有受教育的权利，教育应当免费，至少在初级和基本阶段应如此。初级教育应属义务性质。技术和职业教育应普遍设立。高等教育应根据成绩而对一切人平等开放。

（二）教育的目的在于充分发展人的个性并加强对人权和基本自由的尊重。教育应促进各国、各种族或各宗教集团间的了解、容忍和友谊，并应促进联合国维护和平的各项活动。

（三）父母对其子女所应受的教育的种类，有优先选择的权利。

第二十七条

（一）人人有权自由参加社会的文化生活，享受艺术，并分享科学进步及其产生的福利。

（二）人人对由于他所创作的任何科学、文学或美术作品而产生的精神的和物质的利益，有享受保护的权利。

第二十八条

人人有权要求一种社会的和国际的秩序，在这种秩序中，本宣言所载的权利和自由能获得充分实现。

第二十九条

（一）人人对社会负有义务，因为只有在社会中他的个性才可能得到自由和充分的发展。

（二）人人在行使他的权利和自由时，只受法律所确定的限制，确定此种限制的唯一目的在于保证对旁人的权利和自由给予应有的承认和尊重，并在一个民主的社会中适应道德、公共秩序和普遍福利的正当需要。

（三）这些权利和自由的行使，无论在任何情形下均不得违背联合国的宗旨和原则。

第三十条

本宣言的任何条文，不得解释为默许任何国家、集团或个人有权进行任何旨在破坏本宣言所载的任何权利和自由的活动或行为。

Всеобщая декларация прав человека

ПРЕАМБУЛА

<u>Принимая во внимание</u>, что признание достоинства, присущего всем членам человеческой семьи, и равных и неотъемлемых прав их является основой свободы, справедливости и всеобщего мира; и

<u>принимая во внимание</u>, что пренебрежение и презрение к правам человека привели к варварским актам, которые возмущают совесть человечества, и что создание такого мира, в котором люди будут иметь свободу слова и убеждений и будут свободны от страха и нужды, провозглашено как высокое стремление людей;

<u>принимая во внимание</u>, что необходимо, чтобы права человека охранялись властью закона в целях обеспечения того, чтобы человек не был вынужден прибегать, в качестве последнего средства, к восстанию против тирании и угнетения; и

<u>принимая во внимание</u>, что необходимо содействовать развитию дружественных отношений между народами; и

<u>принимая во внимание</u>, что народы Объединенных Наций подтвердили в Уставе свою веру в основные права человека, в достоинство и ценность человеческой личности и в равноправие мужчин и женщин и решили содействовать социальному прогрессу и улучшению условий жизни при большей свободе; и

<u>принимая во внимание</u>, что государства-члены обязались содействовать, в сотрудничестве с Организацией Объединенных Наций, всеобщему уважению и соблюдению прав человека и основных свобод; и

<u>принимая во внимание</u>, что всеобщее понимание характера этих прав и свобод имеет огромное значение для полного выполнения этого обязательства,

<u>Генеральная Ассамблея</u>

<u>провозглашает</u> настоящую Всеобщую декларацию прав человека в качестве задачи, к выполнению которой должны стремиться все народы и все государства, с тем, чтобы каждый человек и каждый

орган общества, постоянно имея в виду настоящую Декларацию, стремились путем просвещения и образования содействовать уважению этих прав и свобод и обеспечению, путем национальных и международных прогрессивных мероприятий, всеобщего и эффективного признания и осуществления их как среди народов государств - членов Организации, так и среди народов территорий, находящихся под их юрисдикцией.

Статья 1

Все люди рождаются свободными и равными в своем достоинстве и правах. Они наделены разумом и совестью и должны поступать в отношении друг друга в духе братства.

Статья 2

Каждый человек должен обладать всеми правами и всеми свободами, провозглашенными настоящей Декларацией, без какого бы то ни было различия, как то в отношении расы, цвета кожи, пола, языка, религии, политических или иных убеждений, национального или социального происхождения, имущественного, сословного или иного положения.

Кроме того, не должно проводиться никакого различия на основе политического, правового или международного статуса страны или территории, к которой человек принадлежит, независимо от того, является ли эта территория независимой, подопечной, несамоуправляющейся или как-либо иначе ограниченной в своем суверенитете.

Статья 3

Каждый человек имеет право на жизнь, на свободу и на личную неприкосновенность.

Статья 4

Никто не должен содержаться в рабстве или в подневольном состоянии; рабство и работорговля запрещаются во всех их видах.

Статья 5

Никто не должен подвергаться пыткам или жестоким, бесчеловечным или унижающим его достоинство обращению и наказанию.

Статья 6

Каждый человек, где бы он ни находился, имеет право на признание его правосубъектности.

Статья 7

Все люди равны перед законом и имеют право, без всякого различия, на равную защиту закона. Все люди имеют право на равную защиту от какой бы то ни было дискриминации, нарушающей настоящую Декларацию, и от какого бы то ни было подстрекательства к такой дискриминации.

Статья 8

Каждый человек имеет право на эффективное восстановление в правах компетентными национальными судами в случаях нарушения его основных прав, предоставленных ему конституцией или законом.

Статья 9

Никто не может быть подвергнут произвольному аресту, задержанию или изгнанию.

Статья 10

Каждый человек, для определения его прав и обязанностей и для установления обоснованности предъявленного ему уголовного обвинения, имеет право, на основе полного равенства, на то, чтобы его дело было рассмотрено гласно и с соблюдением всех требований справедливости независимым и беспристрастным судом.

Статья 11

1. Каждый человек, обвиняемый в совершении преступления, имеет право считаться невиновным до тех пор, пока его виновность не будет установлена законным порядком путем гласного судебного разбирательства, при котором ему обеспечиваются все возможности для защиты.

2. Никто не может быть осужден за преступление на основании совершения какого-либо деяния или за бездействие, которые во время их совершения не составляли преступления по национальным законам или по международному праву. Не может также налагаться наказание более тяжкое, нежели то, которое могло быть применено в то время, когда преступление было совершено.

Статья 12

Никто не может подвергаться произвольному вмешательству в его личную и семейную жизнь, произвольным посягательствам на неприкосновенность его жилища, тайну его корреспонденции или на его честь и репутацию. Каждый человек имеет право на защиту закона от такого вмешательства или таких посягательств.

Статья 13

1. Каждый человек имеет право свободно передвигаться и выбирать себе местожительство в пределах каждого государства.

2. Каждый человек имеет право покидать любую страну, включая свою собственную, и возвращаться в свою страну.

Статья 14

1. Каждый человек имеет право искать убежища от преследования в других странах и пользоваться этим убежищем.

2. Это право не может быть использовано в случае преследования, в действительности основанного на совершении неполитического преступления, или деяния, противоречащего целям и принципам Организации Объединенных Наций.

Статья 15

1. Каждый человек имеет право на гражданство.

2. Никто не может быть произвольно лишен своего гражданства или права изменить свое гражданство.

Статья 16

1. Мужчины и женщины, достигшие совершеннолетия, имеют право без всяких ограничений по признаку расы, национальности или религии вступать в брак и основывать семью. Они пользуются одинаковыми правами в отношении вступления в брак, во время состояния в браке и во время его расторжения.

2. Брак может быть заключен только при свободном и полном согласии обеих вступающих в брак сторон.

3. Семья является естественной и основной ячейкой общества и имеет право на защиту со стороны общества и государства.

Статья 17

1. Каждый человек имеет право владеть имуществом как единолично, так и совместно с другими.

2. Никто не должен быть произвольно лишен своего имущества.

Статья 18

Каждый человек имеет право на свободу мысли, совести и религии; это право включает свободу менять свою религию или убеждения и свободу исповедовать свою религию или убеждения как единолично, так и сообща с другими, публичным или частным порядком в учении, богослужении и выполнении религиозных и ритуальных порядков.

Статья 19

Каждый человек имеет право на свободу убеждений и на свободное выражение их; это право включает свободу беспрепятственно придерживаться своих убеждений и свободу искать, получать и распространять информацию и идеи любыми средствами и независимо от государственных границ.

Статья 20

1. Каждый человек имеет право на свободу мирных собраний и ассоциаций.

2. Никто не может быть принуждаем вступать в какую-либо ассоциацию.

Статья 21

1. Каждый человек имеет право принимать участие в управлении своей страной непосредственно или через посредство свободно избранных представителей.

2. Каждый человек имеет право равного доступа к государственной службе в своей стране.

3.   Воля народа должна быть основой власти правительства; эта воля должна находить себе выражение в периодических и нефальсифицированных выборах, которые должны проводиться при всеобщем и равном избирательном праве, путем тайного голосования или же посредством других равнозначных форм, обеспечивающих свободу голосования.

Статья 22

Каждый человек, как член общества, имеет право на социальное обеспечение и на осуществление необходимых для поддержания его достоинства и для свободного развития его личности прав в экономической, социальной и культурной областях через посредство национальных усилий и международного сотрудничества и в соответствии со структурой и ресурсами каждого государства.

Статья 23

1.   Каждый человек имеет право на труд, на свободный выбор работы, на справедливые и благоприятные условия труда и на защиту от безработицы.

2.   Каждый человек, без какой-либо дискриминации, имеет право на равную оплату за равный труд.

3.   Каждый работающий имеет право на справедливое и удовлетворительное вознаграждение, обеспечивающее достойное человека существование для него самого и его семьи и дополняемое, при необходимости, другими средствами социального обеспечения.

4.   Каждый человек имеет право создавать профессиональные союзы и входить в профессиональные союзы для защиты своих интересов.

Статья 24

Каждый человек имеет право на отдых и досуг, включая право на разумное ограничение рабочего дня и на оплачиваемый периодический отпуск.

Статья 25

1.   Каждый человек имеет право на такой жизненный уровень, включая пищу, одежду, жилище, медицинский уход и необходимое социальное обслуживание, который необходим для поддержания здоровья и благосостояния его самого и его семьи, и право на обеспечение на случай безработицы, болезни, инвалидности, вдовства, наступления старости или иного случая утраты средств к существованию по не зависящим от него обстоятельствам.

2.   Материнство и младенчество дают право на особое попечение и помощь. Все дети, родившиеся в браке или вне брака, должны пользоваться одинаковой социальной защитой.

Статья 26

1.   Каждый человек имеет право на образование. Образование должно быть бесплатным по меньшей мере в том, что касается начального и общего образования. Начальное образование должно быть обязательным. Техническое и профессиональное образование должно быть общедоступным, и высшее образование должно быть одинаково доступным для всех на основе способностей каждого.

2.   Образование должно быть направлено к полному развитию человеческой личности и к увеличению уважения к правам человека и основным свободам. Образование должно содействовать взаимопониманию, терпимости и дружбе между всеми народами, расовыми и религиозными группами и должно содействовать деятельности Организации Объединенных Наций по поддержанию мира.

3.   Родители имеют право приоритета в выборе вида образования для своих малолетних детей.

Статья 27

1.   Каждый человек имеет право свободно участвовать в культурной жизни общества, наслаждаться искусством, участвовать в научном прогрессе и пользоваться его благами.

2.   Каждый человек имеет право на защиту его моральных и материальных интересов, являющихся результатом научных, литературных или художественных трудов, автором которых он является.

Статья 28

Каждый человек имеет право на социальный и международный порядок, при котором права и свободы, изложенные в настоящей Декларации, могут быть полностью осуществлены.

Статья 29

1. Каждый человек имеет обязанности перед обществом, в котором только и возможно свободное и полное развитие его личности.

2. При осуществлении своих прав и свобод каждый человек должен подвергаться только таким ограничениям, какие установлены законом исключительно с целью обеспечения должного признания и уважения прав и свобод других и удовлетворения справедливых требований морали, общественного порядка и общего благосостояния в демократическом обществе.

3. Осуществление этих прав и свобод ни в коем случае не должно противоречить целям и принципам Организации Объединенных Наций.

Статья 30

Ничто в настоящей Декларации не может быть истолковано как предоставление какому-либо государству, группе лиц или отдельным лицам права заниматься какой-либо деятельностью или совершать действия, направленные к уничтожению прав и свобод, изложенных в настоящей Декларации.

المادة ٢٧

١-   لكل فرد الحق في أن يشترك اشتراكاً حراً في حياة المجتمع الثقافي وفي الاستمتاع بالفنون والمساهمة في التقدم العلمي والاستفادة من نتائجه.

٢-   لكل فرد الحق في حماية المصالح الأدبية والمادية المترتبة على انتاجه العلمي أو الأدبي أو الفني.

المادة ٢٨

لكل فرد الحق في التمتع بنظام اجتماعي دولي تتحقق بمقتضاه الحقوق والحريات المنصوص عليها في هذا الإعلان تحققاً تاماً.

المادة ٢٩

١-   على كل فرد واجبات نحو المجتمع الذي يتاح فيه وحده لشخصيته أن تنمو نمواً حراً كاملاً.

٢-   يخضع الفرد في ممارسة حقوقه وحرياته لتلك القيود التي يقررها القانون فقط، لضمان الاعتراف بحقوق الغير وحرياته واحترامها ولتحقيق المقتضيات العادلة للنظام العام والمصلحة العامة والأخلاق في مجتمع ديمقراطي.

٣-   لا يصح بحال من الأحوال أن تمارس هذه الحقوق ممارسة تتناقض مع أغراض الأمم المتحدة ومبادئها.

المادة ٣٠

ليس في هذا الإعلان نص يجوز تأويله على أنه يخول لدولة أو جماعة أو فرد أي حق في القيام بنشاط أو تأدية عمل يهدف الى هدم الحقوق والحريات الواردة فيه.

المادة ٢٤

لكل شخص الحق في الراحة، وفي أوقات الفراغ، ولا سيما في تحديد معقول لساعات العمل وفي عطلات دورية بأجر.

المادة ٢٥

١- لكل شخص الحق في مستوى من المعيشة كاف للمحافظة على الصحة والرفاهية له ولأسرته، ويتضمن ذلك التغذية والملبس والمسكن والعناية الطبية وكذلك الخدمات الاجتماعية اللازمة، وله الحق في تأمين معيشته في حالات البطالة والمرض والعجز والترمل والشيخوخة وغير ذلك من فقدان وسائل العيش نتيجة لظروف خارجة عن إرادته.

٢- للأمومة والطفولة الحق في مساعدة ورعاية خاصتين، وينعم كل الأطفال بنفس الحماية الاجتماعية سواء أكانت ولادتهم ناتجة عن رباط شرعي أم بطريقة غير شرعية.

المادة ٢٦

١- لكل شخص الحق في التعلم. ويجب أن يكون التعليم في مراحله الأولى والأساسية على الأقل بالمجان. وأن يكون التعليم الأولي إلزامياً. وينبغي أن يعمم التعليم الفني والمهني. وأن ييسر القبول للتعليم العالي على قدم المساواة التامة للجميع وعلى أساس الكفاءة.

٢- يجب أن تهدف التربية الى إنماء شخصية الإنسان إنماء كاملاً. والى تعزيز احترام الإنسان والحريات الأساسية وتنمية التفاهم والتسامح والصداقة بين جميع الشعوب والجماعات العنصرية أو الدينية، والى زيادة مجهود الأمم المتحدة لحفظ السلام.

٣- للآباء الحق الأول في اختيار نوع تربية أولادهم.

المادة ٢١

١-   لكل فرد الحق في الاشتراك في إدارة الشؤون العامة لبلاده، إما مباشرة وإما بواسطة ممثلين يختارون اختياراً حراً.

٢-   لكل شخص نفس الحق الذي لغيره في تقلد الوظائف العامة في البلاد.

٣-   إن إرادة الشعب هي مصدر سلطة الحكومة، ويعبر عن هذه الارادة بانتخابات نزيهة دورية تجري على أساس الاقتراع السري وعلى قدم المساواة بين الجميع أو حسب أي إجراء مماثل يضمن حرية التصويت.

المادة ٢٢

١-   لكل شخص بصفته عضواً في المجتمع الحق في الضمانة الاجتماعية وفي أن تحقق بوساطة المجهود القومي والتعاون الدولي وبما يتفق ونظم كل دولة ومواردها الحقوق الاقتصادية والاجتماعية والتربوية التي لا غنى عنها لكرامته وللنمو الحر لشخصيته.

المادة ٢٣

١-   لكل شخص الحق في العمل، وله حرية اختياره بشروط عادلة مرضية كما أن له حق الحماية من البطالة.

٢-   لكل فرد دون أي تمييز الحق في أجر متساو للعمل.

٣-   لكل فرد يقوم بعمل الحق في أجر عادل مرض يكفل له ولأسرته عيشة لائقة بكرامة الإنسان تضاف اليه، عند اللزوم، وسائل أخرى للحماية الاجتماعية.

٤-   لكل شخص الحق في أن ينشئ وينضم الى نقابات حماية لمصلحته.

المادة ١٦

١- للرجل والمرأة متى بلغا سن الزواج حق التزوج وتأسيس أسرة دون أي قيد بسبب الجنس أو الدين، ولهما حقوق متساوية عند الزواج وأثناء قيامه وعند انحلاله.

٢- لا يبرم عقد الزواج إلا برضى الطرفين الراغبين في الزواج رضى كاملاً لا إكراه فيه.

٣- الأسرة هي الوحدة الطبيعية الأساسية للمجتمع ولها حق التمتع بحماية المجتمع والدولة.

المادة ١٧

١- لكل شخص حق التملك بمفرده أو بالاشتراك مع غيره.

٢- لا يجوز تجريد أحد من ملكه تعسفاً.

المادة ١٨

لكل شخص الحق في حرية التفكير والضمير والدين. ويشمل هذا الحق حرية تغيير ديانته أو عقيدته، وحرية الإعراب عنهما بالتعليم والممارسة وإقامة الشعائر ومراعاتها سواء أكان ذلك سراً أم مع الجماعة.

المادة ١٩

لكل شخص الحق في حرية الرأي والتعبير. ويشمل هذا الحق حرية اعتناق الآراء دون أي تدخل، واستقاء الأنباء والأفكار وتلقيها وإذاعتها بأية وسيلة كانت دون تقيد بالحدود الجغرافية.

المادة ٢٠

١- لكل شخص الحق في حرية الاشتراك في الجمعيات والجماعات السلمية.

٢- لا يجوز إرغام أحد على الانضمام الى جمعية ما.

المادة ١١

١- كل شخص متهم بجريمة يعتبر بريئاً الى أن تثبت ادانته قانوناً بمحاكمة علنية تؤمن له فيها الضمانات الضرورية للدفاع عنه.

٢- لا يدان أي شخص من جراء أداء عمل أو الامتناع عن أداء عمل إلاّ إذا كان ذلك يعتبر جرماً وفقاً للقانون الوطني أو الدولي وقت الارتكاب، كذلك لا توقع عليه عقوبة أشد من تلك التي كان يجوز توقيعها وقت ارتكاب الجريمة.

المادة ١٢

لا يعرض أحد لتدخل تعسفي في حياته الخاصة أو أسرته أو مسكنه أو مراسلاته أو لحملات على شرفه وسمعته، ولكل شخص الحق في حماية القانون من مثل هذا التدخل أو تلك الحملات.

المادة ١٣

١- لكل فرد حرية التنقل واختيار محل اقامته داخل حدود كل دولة.

٢- يحق لكل فرد أن يغادر اية بلاد بما في ذلك بلده كما يحق له العودة اليه.

المادة ١٤

١- لكل فرد الحق في أن يلجأ الى بلاد أخرى أو يحاول الالتجاء اليها هرباً من الاضطهاد.

٢- لا ينتفع بهذا الحق من قدم للمحاكمة في جرائم غير سياسية أو لأعمال تناقض أغراض الأمم المتحدة ومبادئها.

المادة ١٥

١- لكل فرد حق التمتع بجنسية ما.

٢- لا يجوز حرمان شخص من جنسيته تعسفاً أو إنكار حقه في تغييرها.

المادة ٤

لا يجوز استرقاق أو استعباد أي شخص. ويحظر الاسترقاق وتجارة الرقيق بكافة أوضاعهما.

المادة ٥

لا يعرض أي إنسان للتعذيب ولا للعقوبات أو المعاملات القاسية أو الوحشية أو الحاطة بالكرامة.

المادة ٦

لكل إنسان اينما وجد الحق في أن يعترف بشخصيته القانونية.

المادة ٧

كل الناس سواسية أمام القانون ولهم الحق في التمتع بحماية متكافئة عنه دون أية تفرقة. كما أن لهم جميعاً الحق في حماية متساوية ضد أي تميز يخل بهذا الإعلان وضد أي تحريض على تمييز كهذا.

المادة ٨

لكل شخص الحق في أن يلجأ الى المحاكم الوطنية لانصافه عن أعمال فيها اعتداء على الحقوق الأساسية التي يمنحها له القانون.

المادة ٩

لا يجوز القبض على أي إنسان أو حجزه أو نفيه تعسفاً.

المادة ١٠

لكل إنسان الحق، على قدم المساواة التامة مع الآخرين، في أن تنظر قضيته أمام محكمة مستقلة نزيهة نظراً عادلاً علنياً للفصل في حقوقه والتزاماته وأية تهمة جنائية توجه اليه.

فإن الجمعية العامة

تنادي بهذا الإعلان العالمي لحقوق الإنسان

على أنه المستوى المشترك الذي ينبغي أن تستهدفه كافة الشعوب والأمم حتى يسعى كل فرد وهيئة في المجتمع، واضعين على الدوام هذا الإعلان نصب أعينهم، الى توطيد احترام هذه الحقوق والحريات عن طريق التعليم والتربية واتخاذ إجراءات مطردة، قومية وعالمية، لضمان الاعتراف بها ومراعاتها بصورة عالمية فعالة بين الدول الأعضاء ذاتها وشعوب البقاع الخاضعة لسلطانها.

المادة ١

يولد جميع الناس أحراراً متساوين في الكرامة والحقوق. وقد وهبوا عقلاً وضميراً وعليهم أن يعامل بعضهم بعضاً بروح الإخاء.

المادة ٢

لكل إنسان حق التمتع بكافة الحقوق والحريات الواردة في هذا الإعلان، دون أي تمييز، كالتمييز بسبب العنصر أو اللون أو الجنس أو اللغة أو الدين أو الرأي السياسي أو أي رأي آخر، أو الأصل الوطني أو الاجتماعي أو الثروة أو الميلاد أو أي وضع آخر، دون أية تفرقة بين الرجال والنساء.

وفضلاً عما تقدم فلن يكون هناك أي تمييز أساسه الوضع السياسي أو القانوني أو الدولي لبلد أو البقعة التي ينتمي اليها الفرد سواء كان هذا البلد أو تلك البقعة مستقلاً أو تحت الوصاية أو غير متمتع بالحكم الذاتي أو كانت سيادته خاضعة لأي قيد من القيود.

المادة ٣

لكل فرد الحق في الحياة والحرية وسلامة شخصه.

الإعلان العالمي لحقوق الإنسان (أ)

الديباجة

لما كان الاعتراف بالكرامة المتأصلة في جميع أعضاء الأسرة البشرية وبحقوقهم المتساوية الثابتة هو أساس الحرية والعدل والسلام في العالم.

ولما كان تناسي حقوق الإنسان وازدراؤها قد أفضيا الى أعمال همجية آذت الضمير الإنساني، وكان غاية ما يرنو اليه عامة البشر انبثاق عالم يتمتع فيه الفرد بحرية القول والعقيدة ويتحرر من الفزع والفاقة.

ولما كان من الضروري أن يتولى القانون حماية حقوق الإنسان لكيلا يضطر المرء آخر الأمر الى التمرد على الاستبداد والظلم.

ولما كانت شعوب الأمم المتحدة قد أكدت في الميثاق من جديد ايمانها بحقوق الإنسان الأساسية وبكرامة الفرد وقدره وبما للرجال والنساء من حقوق متساوية وحزمت أمرها على أن تدفع بالرقي الاجتماعي قدماً وأن ترفع مستوى الحياة في جو من الحرية أفسح.

ولما كانت الدول الأعضاء قد تعهدت بالتعاون مع الأمم المتحدة على ضمان إطراد مراعاة حقوق الإنسان والحريات الأساسية واحترامها.

ولما كان للإدراك العام لهذه الحقوق والحريات الأهمية الكبرى للوفاء التام بهذا التعهد.

(أ)   اعتُمد بموجب قرار الجمعية العامة ٢١٧ ألف(د-٣) المؤرخ في ١٠ كانون الأول/ديسمبر ١٩٤٨.